Yiddish Wisdom
for Marriage

✴

Library of Congress Cataloging-in-Publication Data available.

ISBN 0-8118-3281-3

Note on the translation and transliteration:
Translation is the process of turning or rendering one language into another. Transliteration is the process of rendering phonetically the sound of one language with the letters of another language. The transliterated words in this volume are a very close approximation to the pronunciation of Yiddish words using the system developed by the YIVO (Yiddish Scientific Institute). The acronym YIVO is a transliteration of the first letters in the four Yiddish words that make up the name of the organization.
—R.M.

Printed in Hong Kong

Designed by Brenna Ramirez

Distributed in Canada by
Raincoast Books
9050 Shaughnessy Street
Vancouver, British Columbia V6P 6E5

10 9 8 7 6 5 4 3 2 1

Chronicle Books LLC
85 Second Street
San Francisco, California 94105

www.chroniclebooks.com

Yiddish Wisdom
for Marriage

※ *Yiddishe Khokhme far Khasene*

TRANSLATION AND INTRODUCTION BY
Rae Meltzer

ILLUSTRATIONS BY
Kristina Swarner

CHRONICLE BOOKS

SAN FRANCISCO

Introduction |

O MAKE THESE LOVED COMPANIONS REJOICE, AS OF
OLD IN THE GARDEN OF EDEN.
— *traditional wedding benediction*

The wedding in Jewish custom and folklore is a great celebration, with klezmer music, dancing, drinking, feasting, with the canopy, or *khupe,* as the focal point of the ceremony. Here, the bride and groom pledge their commitment to each other and receive the traditional blessings. They exchange rings, the groom crushes a glass beneath his foot, and then the merrymaking starts as the couple begin the rest of their lives together.

Proverbs are located throughout Jewish literature, including the Old Testament, which regards marriage as the means to true companionship. For example; we discover the addage, "He who finds a wife finds a great good" [Prov. 18:22]; and the admonition, "Live joyfully with your wife whom you love" [Eccles. 9:9].

The proverbs collected in this book reflect the centrality of marriage and the bond between married partners in the Jewish family. They focus on the love, joy, and responsibility of bride and groom toward one another, and their obligation to cherish, respect, protect, and understand.

Yiddish developed a thousand years ago in Europe from a blend of Hebrew fragments and local German and Slavic dialects. With the migration of its speakers, it also absorbed words from neighboring languages such as Russian, Polish, Czechoslovakian, Latvian, Lithuanian, and other European tongues. Although Yiddish and Hebrew use the same characters, each language has a separate vocabulary, history, and linguistic structure.

Today, there's a renaissance of interest in Yiddish in Jewish communities as well as on college campuses, where courses in the language are offered more and more frequently. And just as Yiddish has roots in many languages, Yiddish words and expressions have found a home in American English, through words such as *mentsh* (mature person), *maven* (expert), *shlep* (to drag), and *beygl* (bagel).

Yiddish proverbs have been passed along in an oral tradition for generations and finally collected and preserved in writing about one hundred years ago. In these proverbs about living a happily married life there is wit, humor, and earthy folk wisdom that reflect the rich history of the Jewish people and the vibrant color of the Yiddish language.

–Rae Meltzer

Even in Heaven it is not good to
be alone; better to be a pair.

*Afile in gan-eydn iz oykh nit gut tzu zayn aleyn; es
iz beser tzu zayn a por.*

✵

Early to rise and early to wed,
no harm done.

Free oyfshteyn un free khasene hobn, shat nit.

꽃

You and I are a happy pair;
without you I fizzle out and
amount to nothing.

*Ikh mit dir zaynen a gliklekhe por; on dir plots ikh
un ikh bin gornisht.*

꽃

When a couple fights, it cools
their anger.

Az me beyzert zikh on geyt op der kaas.

꽃

Delay is good for cheese, but not for a wedding.

Opleygn iz nor gut for kez, ober nit far a khasene.

✳

If a slice of bread falls buttered-side down, it means that the bride is hungry.

Az dos broyt falt mit der puter arop, iz a simen az di kale iz hungerik.

✳

The husband who doesn't believe in God should have a devout wife.

Ver gleybt nit in Got darf hobn a frum vayb.

✳

A home without a wife is like a
wagon without wheels.

A shtub on a vayb iz vi a vogn on reder.

�֍

Better to lose with a wise man
than to win with a fool.

*Beser mit a klugn tsu farlirn eyder mit a nar tsu
gevinen.*

�֍

A couple's quarrel is like an itch;
the more they scratch, the more
it itches.

*A gekrig iz vi a baysenish; vos mer men kratst, alts
mer bayst es.*

✤

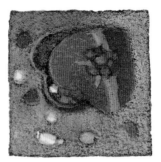

If the groom doesn't please
the bride, his gifts don't please
her either.

*Az der khosn gefelt nit der kale, gefeln zayne matones
oykh nit.*

※

A man should ask for three things: a good wife, a good year, and a good dream.

Der man zol betn far dray zakhn: a gute vayb, a gutn yor, un a gutn kholem.

❖

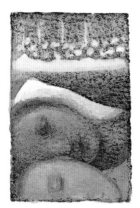

There is no one more devoted than one's wife.

Es iz nito kayner vos iz mer ibergegebn vi di eygene vayb.

✻

There are no secrets from one's wife.

Fun di eygene vayb iz nito kayn soydes.

✳

Good will toward others is the best charity.

Der guter viln iz di beste tsdoke.

✳

If the will is strong, one will achieve it.

Az der viln iz shtark, vet men es dergreykhn.

✳

When the bride and groom are kissing, the matchmakers can go home.

Ven khosn-kale kushn zikh shoyn, megn di shatkhonim geyn aheym.

✳

The mother says to the hurt child,
  "By the time you are a bride
  (or groom), it will be healed."

*Zogt di mame tsu ir tsemazekt kind, "Biz du vest a
  khosn [oder a kale] vern, vet es zikh oysheyln."*

❋

Between wife and husband, words
  should be weighed, not counted.

Tsvishn vayb un man, dorf men verter vegn, nit tseyln.

❋

When he loves his wife, he also
  loves her family.

Az men hot lib dos vayb hot men oykh lib ir mishpokhe.

❋

When the wife is like a queen,
the husband is like a king.

Az dos vayb iz a malke, iz der man a meylekh.

❀

Wives can lead to good or mislead,
but either way, they lead.

*Vayber firn tsum gutn oder tsum beyzn, say vi say,
farfirn zey.*

❀

He wants the moon from the sky.

Er vil di levone fun dem himl.

✻

If it is not what one wishes, then
one must want what it is.

Az es iz nit vos me vil, muz men veln vos es makht
zikh.

✳

Not all that you know may you say.

Nit alts vos du veyst megst du zogn.

✳

Two things must be protected:
a bride and a groom.

Tsvey zakhn muz men bavorenen: a kale un a khosn.

✳

There are things that a wife must
not show even to her husband.

*Es zenen zakhn vos men tor afile dem eygenem man
nit vayzn.*

※

Weigh advice from friends, but
decide for yourself.

*Batrakht di eytse fun fraynt, ober makh dayn
eygenem bashlus.*

※

Don't be too sweet, or they will
eat you up; don't be too bitter, or
they will spit you out.

*Zay nit tsu zis, me zol dikh nit oyfesn; zay nit tsu
biter, men zol dikh nit oys-shpayen.*

※

Intimacy is good only with
one's wife.

Intimkayt iz gut nor mit di eygene vayb.

※

A dream is half a prophecy.

A kholem iz a halb nevue.

※

Someone who finds fault with
everything will complain that
the bride is too beautiful.

*Di kale iz tsu sheyn, zogt eyner was gefint a khisorn
mit altsding.*

✳

A married daughter is like bread
sliced from the loaf; she can't be
reattached to her parents.

*An oysgegebene tokhter iz vi an opgeshnitn shtik
broyt; zi ken zikh shoyn mer nit tzurik tsuklepn tsu
di eltern.*

✳

Why does the bear dance?
Because he doesn't have a wife.

Farvos tanst der ber? Vayl er hot nit kayn vayb.

✳

The divine presence shines His
blessing upon all brides.

Oyf ale kales shaynen di brokhe fun di shkhine.

※

With a meat stew as with an
engaged couple, one does not
look too closely.

In a tsholnt un in a shidukh kukt men nit tsufil arayn.

☼

Passion and desire have an
iron will.

Der yeytser-ho're hot an ayzenem viln.

☼

Under the veil all brides are beautiful.

Unter dektikhl zaynen ale kales sheyn.

Although the bride is bashful and
coy, she likes her fun.

Di kale shemt zikh take, ober hanoe hot zi.

✵

There is no unattractive bride,
and no cantor who sings badly at
weddings.

*Es iz nito kayn miese kale, un nito kayn khazn vos
zingt shlekht tzu der khasene.*

❋

The bride always wants her new
family to be like her own family.

*Fun vos far a mishpokhe di kale kumt aroys, in aza
mishpokhe, vintsht zi vider arayntsukumen.*

❋

Praise me and I praise you;
we belong to the same union.

*Loyb du mikh un ikh vel loybn dikh; beyde zenen mir
fun eyn tsekh.*

❋

Not what is beautiful is loved,
but what is loved is beautiful.

Nit dos vos iz sheyn iz lib, nor dos vos iz lib, iz sheyn.

※

**Love me a little, but love
me always.**

Hob mikh veynik lib, nor hob mikh lang lib.

※

**When an old man marries a
young woman, he gets younger
and she gets older.**

*Az an alter man nemt a yunge vayb, vert der man
yung un dos vayb alt.*

※

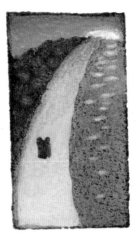

**Where there is love and affection
it is never too crowded or lonely.**

*Vu es iz libshaft un varemkayt dort iz kayn mol
engshaft oder elentkayt.*

Their relationship is like the
sun and the moon, who pass
each other by.

*Zeyer batsyung iz vi di zun un di levone, zey iberyogn
yeder anderer.*

✻

Between husband and wife only
God can judge.

Tsvishn man un vayb iz nor Got a shoyfet.

✳

Husband and wife are of one
body, but they have separate
pockets for their cash.

*Man un vayb zaynen eyn leyb ober keshenes hobn
zey tsvey.*

✳

Silence is the fence around wisdom.

Shtilkayt iz di fartsamung arum khokhme.

✳

Marriage makes an old maid a
young wife.

Nokh der khasene vert on alt meydl a yunge vaybl.

✺

Little girls break toys; big girls
break your heart.

*Kleyne meydlekh tsubrekhn di tsatskes; groyse
meydlekh tsubrekhn di harts.*

✺

You can't dance at two weddings
at the same time.

Me ken nit tantsn oyf tsvey khasenes in der zelber tsayt.

✺

They live together like two turtle doves.

Zey lebn tsuzamen vi tsvey toybn.

✺

Let us talk about more cheerful things.

Lomir redn fun freylekhe zakhn.

✳

Better a little luck than a lot of gold.

Beser a bisl mazl eyder a sakh gold.

※

Luck doesn't stay around, so use it without delay.

Dos mazl lozt nit lang mit zikh shpiln; darf men es glaykh nutsn.

※

When one needs brains, brawn won't help.

Ven men darf hobn moyekh, helft nit kayn koyekh.

※

Parents can give a dowry, but they can't give luck.

Eltern kenen gebn nadn, ober zey kenen nit gebn mazl.

❋

God gives us two ears and one mouth so we can hear more and talk less.

Got hot gegebn dem mentshn tsvey oyern un eyn moyl az der mentsh zol mer hern un veyniker redn.

❋

**By day they're ready for divorce,
by night they're ready for bed.**

Bay tog tsum get, bay nakht tsum bet.

❇

**One who is no good to himself is
no good to anyone.**

Eyner ver iz nit gut tsu zikh iz nit gut tsu yenem.

❇

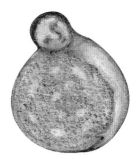

If you want to, you can move the whole world.

Az me vil, ken men iberkern di gantse velt.

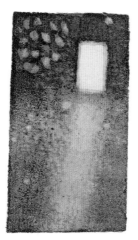

**When you fight, leave the door
open for making up.**

*Az du krigst zikh, krig zikh azoy az du zolst zikh
kenen iberbetn.*

❖

Goodness is better than piety.

Gutskayt iz beser fun frumkayt.

＊

The first fight is the best fight.

Der ershter broygez iz der bester broygez.

＊

**When you speak from your heart,
you feel better.**

Az me redt zikh arop fun hartsn, vert gringer.

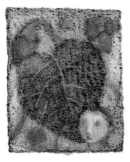

It's good to look upon a beautiful person, but it's better to live with a smart one.

Oyf a sheynem perzon iz gut tsu kukn, mit a klugn iz gut tsu lebn.

✻

When the heart is full, the eyes overflow.

Az dos harts iz ful, veln di oygn aribergisn.

✻

You can catch more flies with honey than with vinegar.

Mit honik ken men khapn mer flign vi mit esik.

❈

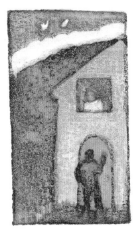

When the destined groom arrives,
the bride quickly decides.

Az der khosn iz der basherter, darf di kale nit
kayn verter.

✳

**Better to break an engagement
than a marriage.**

Beser di t'no'im tseraysn eyder di ksube.

☀

**If you're faithful to your wife,
you'll have a healthy life.**

*Az du bist getray tsu dayn vayb, vest du hobn a
gezuntn lebn.*

☀

**Desire is asleep in a maiden,
but awake in a wife.**

*Der yeytser-ho're shloft bay a meydl, un iz vakh
bay a vaybl.*

☀

It is better to be embarrassed than
heartbroken.

Es iz beser farshemen zikh in ponim, eyder a
tsebrokhn harts.

✵

Let's talk with a purpose, as
between friends.

Lomir redn takhlis, vi tsvishn fraynt.

✵

As friends, let's live and let live.

Alts fraynt darf men lebn un lozn lebn.

✵

**If there's a will, there's a way;
you just have to want to do it.**

*Oyb me vil can men gefinen a veg; me darf nor
veln dos ton.*

✻

**Why does a bride who looks
forward happily to her wedding
begin to weep as she walks to
the canopy?**

*Vi farshteyt men a meydl vos vart mit freyd
oyf ir khosen un ir khosene un veynt az zi geyt
tsu der khupe?*

✻

Silence is golden.

Shvaygn iz gold'n.

✺

A pretty girl stirs a boy's desire.

A sheyne meydl vet oyfvekn a bokher's glust.

※

**A girl doesn't have to be pretty if
she has charm.**

A meydl darf nit zayn sheyn eyb zi hot kheyn.

※

**It doesn't cost anything to
promise love.**

Tsuzogn libe kost nit kayn gelt.

✳

**When the bride is refined, the
wife is a little dove.**

Ven di meydl iz eydl, iz di vaybl a taybl.

✳

**What the eye doesn't see,
the heart doesn't know.**

Vos di oyg zet nit, di harts veys nit.

✳

The bride pinches her cheeks to
make them pink when she stands
under the canopy.

Di kale knaypt di bakn, abi di farb zol shteyn ven zi
iz unter der khupe.

☀

Keep on trying and you will be happy.

Me dreyt zikh un me freyt zikh.

✺

That's how the cookie crumbles.

Azoy vert dos kikhl tsebrokhn.

✺

Like soap for the body, so are
tears for the soul.

Vi zeyf farn guf, azoy zaynen trern far der neshome.

※

After nine months the secret
comes out.

Nokh nine hadoshim kumt der sod aroys.

※

It's not the pretty face, but the
good heart that's important.

Nit dos sheyne ponim iz der iker, nor dos sheyne harts.

※

The face tells the secret.

Dos ponim zogt oys dem sod.

✻

Making a living depends on the husband's luck, and rearing children depends on the wife's.

Parnose iz inem man's mazl, kinder zaynen inem vayb's mazl.

✻

Only a stone should be alone.

Nor a shteyn zol zayn aleyn.

✳

**To our friendship; may we live
long and laugh often.**

Tsu unzer frayntshaft; lomir lebn lang un lakhn oft.

�֎

You should live and be well.

Du zolst lebn un gezunt zayn.

✷

Wisdom is better than riches.

Khokhme iz beser fun raykhkayt.

✷

Wisdom is precious.

Khokhme iz tayer.

✻

**Life is the greatest bargain;
we get it for nothing.**

Dos lebn iz di greste metsie; men krigt dos umzist.

✻

**If one has luck one can do
anything.**

Alts ken men ton eyb me hot mazl.

✻

**A husband doesn't have to be tall
to be great.**

A man darf nit zayn hoykh tsu zayn groys.

Better to make a good wish
for yourself than a bad wish
for another.

Beser tzu makhn a gutn vintsh far zikh eyder a
shlekhtn vintsh far yenem.

☼

Keep yourself in mind and you
will forget the unpleasantness
of others.

*Hob zikh in zinen vest du fargesn on yene vos
zaynen beyz.*

※

A husband is what he is, not what
he has been.

A man iz vos er iz, nit vos er iz geven.

※

The joy is greater when the crowd is smaller.

Di freyd iz greser ven der oylem iz klener.

✷

**A husband is sometimes as strong
as iron, sometimes as weak as a fly.**

*A man iz a mol shtarker fun ayzn, un a mol shlof
vi a flig.*

※

**He who asks for directions doesn't
get lost.**

Er vos fregt di onfirung farblondzshet nit.

※

**The tongue is a person's
greatest enemy.**

Di tsung iz dem mentshn's grester soyne.

※

**You can't make cheesecakes
out of snow.**

Gomolkes ken men nit makhn fun shney.

❋

Where you need sugar, salt won't do.

Vu me darf hobn tsuker, toyg nit kayn zalts.

�֍

Time is the best healer.

Di tsayt iz der bester dokter.

✖

Time is more precious than money.

Di tsayt iz tayerer fun gelt.

✖

A joke is a half-truth.

A kotoves iz a halber emes.

✳

Whoever eats lots of pudding will live a long time.

Ver es est lang kugl lebt lang.

✳

Rich relatives are close; poor ones are distant.

Raykhe kroyvim zaynen noent; oreme kroyvim vayt.

✳

**A mother-in-law forgets that
she was once a daughter-in-law.**

*Di shviger fargest az zi iz a mol aleyn geven
a shnur.*

✼

**Silence is good, but speech is
even better.**

Shvaygn iz gut, redn iz nokh beser.

✼

**For the sake of peace one may
even tell a lie.**

Fun sholem vegn meg men afile a lign zogn.

✼

Easy love, heavy damage.

Laykhte libe, shvere hezek.

✬

**When you enjoy a friend's
wedding, you'll live to enjoy
your own.**

*Az me freyt zikh mit yenem's khasene derlebt men
di eygene.*

✬

It's never too late to get married.

Es iz keyn mol nit tsu shpet khasene hobn.

※

After the wedding it's too late to have regrets.

Nokh der khasene iz tsu shpet di kharote.

※

Prayers go up to heaven; blessings come down to earth.

Di tfiles geyen aroyf tsum himl; un di brokhes geyen arop tsum erd.

☀